an ePoet® production

S. E. Harrison

PLUTONOMICS
A Unified Theory of Wealth

an Inventerprise® book
published by ePoet®

Copyright © 2006 by S. E. Harrison.

Published by ePoet LLC
Los Angeles, California
www.epoet.com

Manufactured in the United States of America.

Library of Congress Control Number: 2006903925

Publisher's Cataloging-In-Publication Data
(Prepared by The Donohue Group, Inc.)

Harrison, S. E.
    Plutonomics : a unified theory of wealth / S.E. Harrison.

    p. : ill. ; cm. -- (an Inventerprise book)

    ISBN: 0-9776420-0-3

    1. Wealth. 2. Distribution (Economic theory) 3. Finance, Personal. I. Title

HB251 .H37 2006
330.1/6

To my teachers and students

Contents

Introduction

The Aim for this Book

Plutonomics: A Unified Theory of Wealth presents a brief, simple overview of the factors and nature of wealth. The text is divided into two sections. The first section describes and discusses each of the factors of wealth and how they interact. The second section highlights basic principles for enhancing wealth.

The work as a whole is intended to provide an intellectual foundation for theoretical inquiry into and practical mastery of the concept of wealth.

Who Might Enjoy this Book

Plutonomics: A Unified Theory of Wealth is directed primarily toward two groups of readers: (i) individuals who wish not only to maximize their own wealth but also to understand it, to gain a conceptual foundation upon which to build wealth; and (ii) students and theorists in the fields of economics, business and finance who have become disillusioned with the conventional views in these fields and increasingly dissatisfied with the real-world consequences of these views.

Many individuals in the first group find the enormous volume of print and electronic publications addressing the topic of wealth to be daunting. There are literally thousands of books and Web sites proffering wealth advice, and sorting through this material can be exhausting and unrewarding. A large portion of the information one finds is duplicative, and much of the rest is contradictory.

What seems to be absent from this mass, however, is a philosophical framework comprehensive and cohesive enough to relate wealth to the broader concerns of simply leading a good, happy life. *Plutonomics: A Unified Theory of Wealth* offers such a framework.

Students and theorists in the second group typically find many of the prevailing theories in economics, business and finance unpersuasive intellectually and destructive practically. For instance, growing recognition of the drawbacks of treating gross domestic product (GDP) as a measure of anything worth measuring manifests itself in a number of proposed alternatives — e.g., GPI (genuine progress indicator), GNH (gross national happiness) — that are intended to depict societal wealth more meaningfully and realistically.

But opponents of the conventional wisdom too often try to fight fire with fire, hoping to overcome flawed economics with slightly-less-flawed economics. Environmentalists currently lead that charge, and, while their labors are noble and admirable, these efforts may never come to fruition unless a compelling alternative theoretical basis comes forth, one that not only comprises economics but also grasps and explains that which economics cannot. *Plutonomics: A Unified Theory of Wealth* offers such a basis.

How to Use this Book

This book is fully integrated with a website located at www.plutonomics.com.

Supplementary materials include:

bibliography
plutonomics.com/bibliography

glossary
plutonomics.com/glossary

origins of plutonomics
plutonomics.com/origins

index
plutonomics.com/book-index

Please also send your insights, comments, suggestions, questions and criticism through the website.

plutonomics.com

Background

Of the great human obsessions, wealth may be second only to love in terms of the fervor it inspires. Both pursuits spur suitors to new heights and new depths, precipitate wars and treachery, and inspire sermon writers and storytellers.

But unlike love, which may forever remain magically unknowable — and we can be thankful for poets, if so —, wealth seems to be a topic that would lend itself to analysis and, eventually, reduction to a practical manual. Wealth should be knowable — and known.

So went the reasoning, anyway, that first led me to begin searching for a basic, modern handbook of wealth, some kind of plainspoken document that said, "This is wealth, and this is what you do to get it." But that search turned out to be very disappointing. Surprisingly — and it still surprises —, such a book could hardly be found.

The exploration began with the theories of the major economists, since they seemed to be a natural point of entry. But it soon became clear that what we mean by wealth exceeds the scope of economics, that wealth involves more than just goods and services, market transactions and resource allocation.

The search soon broadened to include the work of philosophers and get-rich authors, but it continued to disappoint. The topic merited something more practical than abstract philosophy but more substantial than here-is-a-really-good-mutual-fund. That middle ground proved elusive.

By 1993, disappointment had morphed into mission. If no one else were going to assemble such a book, it must have been my job to do so.

Toward that end, a portion of the general theory of wealth, including a version of capacity (the forerunner of what is now capacity to influence), influence and environment, had been created by 1994. But the more subtle concepts of appreciation and appreciative capacity did not coalesce until at least a year later.

Influenceables, appreciables and inaccessibles took on much of their present form in 1996. By then, it was clear that capacity and appreciation, as used herein, were essentially absent from prior wealth literature and that the various forms of influence had never been brought together under one roof, which absences explain the disappointing search for a handbook.

Nonetheless, neither my intent nor desire had

ever been to work in economics or psychology, and I felt unqualified to draft a document that would be acceptable to the degree that it fell into these fields. Specifically, these fields have come to be dominated by what the present work calls "precision bias," and I definitely felt unprepared to unleash a barrage of statistics sufficient to impress those who trust more in numbers than life. I therefore spent several years researching, writing and rewriting toward the output of a very academic, read, statistics-oriented, presentation of a unified theory of wealth.

During the first ten years, probably six or eight drafts of varying length and quality were written and then completely abandoned, and this cycle may have repeated infinitely were it not for the fortuitous entrance of Danielle Miller.

In 2003, Danielle was taking time off from her legal career and searching for an interesting intellectual activity. We happened to meet and began a discourse of several months that crystallized the theory into something that could be more readily explained. Among other things, through this collaboration, we hammered out the current taxonomy for the forms of appreciation and influence and also the probabilistic and correlative formulae for prospective and retrospective wealth.

A motto emerged during the period of our collaboration, "Choose Better," which phrase — through the double entendre — succinctly embodies the two-part goal of this project.

Even, however, with these pillars in place, which would probably have been more than adequate to enable a superior theorist to write, I was unable to write the book. I wanted numbers. In particular, I wanted numbers that have been sought and not found by a host of philosophers, worldly and otherwise, especially Bentham and the utilitarians, numbers that could be attached to individual experiences, direct — commensurable — pleasure and pain numbers.

In short, I needed to assuage my own precision bias.

In a hidden-in-plain-view way, an unlikely ally "appeared" in March, 2005, having been there all along, to do just that: the English/American common law system. Without design, the blind working of the common law system, having no purpose but to resolve cases and controversies, provides the insight I myself needed in order to overcome my own precision bias.

Specifically, thousands of tort cases each year require thousands of attorneys, litigants, judges and jurors to consider and ultimately assign dollar values to "non-economic damages," such as pain and suffering, loss of consortium, and the like. *While the numbers themselves may be impossible to determine with precision, virtually no one now disputes that numbers can be, should be, must be and are assigned to non-economic, non-transferable qualities.*

This point in turn betrays that the issue is not *whether* these qualities have a wealth value, but simply *how much* wealth value they have. Precision bias restrains us from admitting that actual values — big ones — do indisputably attach to non-transferable forms of wealth. They exist, whether we can precisely quantify them or not. If that be true, then excluding recognizably relevant, weighty factors from the calculations upon which we base wealth decisions is but an arbitrary — and, in my view, wildly misguided and demonstrably detrimental — preference for precision over accuracy.

Viewed in this light, the combined efforts of millions of participants in the common law system over the course of hundreds of years have unwittingly produced a body of wealth-related literature — and numbers — that is unrivaled on a pragmatic level by other fields purporting to address the topic of wealth directly.

Finally, after more than a decade of research and development, the present book basically wrote itself during the week of September 4, 2005, unimpeded by a need for data tables. While but a brief introduction to the basic concepts of plutonomics, it seems minimally adequate for that limited purpose.

During the process, necessity dictated creation of the word **jatalla** (\jə-TÄ-lə\ n — **jatallic** \-lik\ adj), simply because my vocabulary does not include a word that adequately expresses this concept, if such an English word exists. The most relevant prior term in English appears to be "zero-sum," coined in the mid-1900s, which is somewhat of an imperfect antonym for jatalla.

The word "plutonomics" apparently dates back to the 1850s but fell out of use in the 1920s or 30s, probably because of the growing sway of economic thought and the — erroneous — view that plutonomics and economics are the same thing. Meanwhile, a handful of pre-existing English words — wealth, capacity, influence, appreciation and environment — have been conscripted and pressed into service of the present purpose and, when so exploited, capitalized.

The journey into plutonomics has been an exciting one for me. Wealth and the concept of wealth reach into virtually every sphere of human activity, and studying wealth has accordingly led me into a number of fields to which I had previously had little exposure.

This work remains but a tentative launch rather than a definitive landing, and, with its completion, I return — at least for a while — to more familiar realms. However, I hope that *Plutonomics: A Unified Theory of Wealth* will inspire some readers to advance the field of plutonomics and some to develop personal mastery of wealth.

S.E. Harrison
Los Angeles, California

Book I

The Study of Wealth

Part I
1

When a newborn enters the world, all that exists to the newborn is the in-here and the out-there.

In-here consists primarily of feelings, like loneliness, and urges, like hunger.

Out-there consists of everything that can be sensed: that which can be seen and heard, felt and smelled and tasted.

The infant soon learns that satisfying the in-here depends on the out-there.

This learning is the first lesson of Wealth.

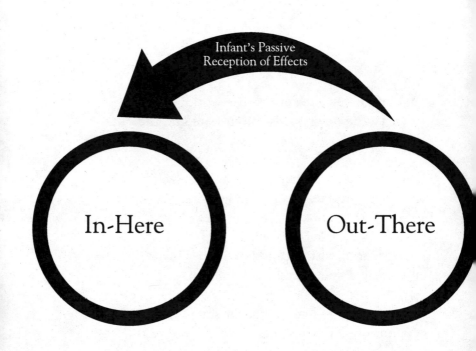

2

At first, in the interaction of in-here and out-there, the infant is very passive.

He or she is picked up by giants and fed milk, then wrapped, unwrapped, wrapped again, carried about, and tucked in.

The in-here receives. The warmth of loving arms, the nourishing breast, the soft cradle, the music of voices — each stimulus out-there falls onto the fertile ground of the in-here.

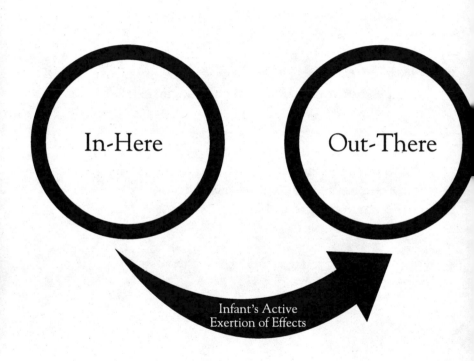

3

But the infant is not entirely passive.

If nothing else, the infant can cry, and this crying often proves to be an effective act of manipulating the out-there to serve the needs of the in-here.

Over time, the infant learns that he or she has this power and need not accept the out-there just as it is, that sometimes the infant can change the out-there to his or her liking.

quotes for comparison

What a piece of work is man! How noble in reason! How infinite in faculty! In form, in moving, how express and admirable! In action how like an angel! In apprehension how like a god! The beauty of the world! The paragon of animals!

William Shakespeare
(1564-1616)
Hamlet

4

In the way of Wealth, the in-here is called *Capacity*. Capacity is the most mysterious of the four factors of Wealth.

It differentiates living creatures from inanimate objects.

It is easy to destroy but impossible to create.

It cannot be bought, borrowed or stolen.

But it can be imparted by one to another, cultivated and expanded.

quotes for comparison

Lay not up for yourselves treasures upon earth, where moth and rust doth corrupt, and where thieves break through and steal. But lay up for yourselves treasures in heaven, where neither moth nor rust doth corrupt, and where thieves do not break through nor steal. For where your treasure is, there will your heart be also.

Jesus Christ
(4 B.C.-29 A.D.)
quoted in The Gospel According to St. Matthew

5

In the way of Wealth, the out-there is called *Environment*.

Environment can only be determined in reference to the particular person whose Wealth is being considered.

To you, I am a part of the out-there, a feature of Environment. To me, you are a feature of Environment.

Thus, Environment is inherently relative and different for everyone.

Many features of Environment — air, water, food — are necessary to survival, the preservation of Capacity.

quotes for comparison

The study of sciences can tame only those who are possessed of such mental faculties as obedience, hearing, grasping, retentive memory, discrimination, inference, and deliberation, but not others devoid of such faculties.

Whoever carries into practice whatever he is taught concerning righteousness and wealth is one of sharp intelligence; whoever never carries into practice the good instructions he has imbibed is one of stagnant intelligence; and whoever entangles himself in dangers and hates righteousness and wealth is one of perverted mind.

Kautalya
(circa 350-275 B.C.)
Arthashastra

6

In the way of Wealth, the effect of the out-there upon the in-here is called *Appreciation*.

Appreciation denotes any process through which the out-there — Environment — actively affects the in-here — Capacity — and the in-here passively receives the effects of the out-there.

Through Appreciation, Environment achieves its most direct and significant impact on Wealth, that of sustaining Capacity.

Digestion, respiration, tasting, seeing and hearing — these are some of many forms of Appreciation, processes through which a human realizes the effects of Environment.

In contrast to the established meaning of the word "appreciation," any effect of Environment upon the person, whether beneficial or detrimental, is called Appreciation for the purposes of Wealth analysis.

However, the type of Appreciation we prefer to have, i.e., beneficial Appreciation, is consonant with the common meaning of the word.

quotes for comparison

There is nothing so degrading as the constant anxiety about one's means of livelihood. I have nothing but contempt for the people who despise money. They are hypocrites or fools. Money is like a sixth sense without which you cannot make a complete use of the other five. Without an adequate income half the possibilities of life are shut off. The only thing to be careful about is that you do not pay more than a shilling for the shilling you earn.

W. Somerset Maugham
(1874-1965)
Of Human Bondage

7

In the way of Wealth, the effect of the in-here upon the out-there is called *Influence*.

Influence denotes any process through which the in-here, Capacity, actively affects the out-there, Environment, or alters the relationship between Capacity and Environment.

In infancy, we quickly discover that life-sustaining Appreciation is far too important to be left entirely to chance, to the whims of Environment.

To protect ourselves from such whims, we independently discover a wide variety of techniques — crying, grabbing, walking — that allow us a certain degree of control over Environment.

Influence is this arsenal of techniques.

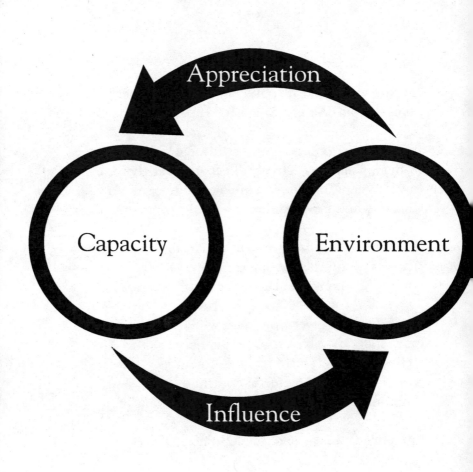

8

These factors, therefore, comprise the manifold of Wealth: Capacity, Environment, Appreciation and Influence. The study of these factors and the ways in which they combine into Wealth is called *plutonomics*.

The nature of each factor of Wealth is very different from that of the other factors, as different as giving is from receiving, action from inaction, living from lifeless.

To know Wealth is to know not only the special nature of each factor but also the ways in which these four factors interact with each other.

Ultimately, if one wishes to enjoy greater Wealth, one should seek to develop mastery of Wealth.

Such mastery requires not only knowledge of Wealth but also the ability and willingness to apply such knowledge.

Part II
9

As a child grows, certain limitations, such as blindness or deafness or inability to tolerate exposure to certain foods or conditions, are readily apparent.

Other limitations may be more difficult to recognize, such as cognitive or personality disorders.

Many limitations may simply be shadows of strengths: inability to maintain attention to a task may be construed as a preference for spontaneity, for instance.

But each child is a unique collection of thousands of such limitations upon Capacity.

quotes for comparison

The reader will find, again, that there is never, in any single instance, an attempt made to compare the amount of feeling in one mind with that in another. I see no means by which such comparison can be accomplished.

W. S. Jevons
(1835-1882)
The Theory of Political Economy

10

Given the central role of Capacity in Wealth, and given that no two individuals have the same Capacity, Wealth can be evaluated only on an individual basis.

In other words, even when all objective conditions are identical, the Wealth of two individuals may nonetheless differ greatly according to their respective levels of Capacity.

Thus, Wealth is inherently *subjective*.

quotes for comparison

Water, water, everywhere,
And all the boards did shrink;
Water, water, everywhere,
Nor any drop to drink.

Samuel Taylor Coleridge
(1772-1834)
The Rime of the Ancient Mariner

11

But even if a child has perfect capacity to see, he or she may have nothing to read.

Even if a child has perfect capacity to digest, he or she may have nothing to eat.

Indeed, even if a child has food to eat but cannot open the container in which the food is stored, the child effectively has nothing to eat.

Thus, Capacity by itself does not ensure that Appreciation will occur.

quotes for comparison

The value of goods arises from their relationship to our needs, and is not inherent in the goods themselves. With changes in this relationship, value arises and disappears.

Carl Menger
(1840-1921)
Principles of Economics

12

Capacity remains but potential Wealth until circumstances allow realization of this potential. Actual Wealth results from coincidence of certain forms of Capacity (e.g., capacity to digest) and suitable features of Environment (e.g., food).

Once the right conditions are met, this indispensable interplay of Capacity and Environment occurs either as Appreciation (e.g., digestion) or Influence (e.g., opening a can).

Thus, Wealth is inherently *contextual*.

quotes for comparison

Wealth unused might as well not exist.

Aesop
(620-560 B.C.)
The Miser and His Gold

13

Once a child is eating and digesting his food, or seeing and reading a book, or breathing or running or laughing — in all these cases, potential has become actual. When Capacity moves from potential to actual, a process results.

That is, potential to do has become doing, a process that begins happening at one point in time and ceases happening at another point in time.

A process cannot both halt and proceed.

In other words, processes do not so much "exist" as "occur," and they only occur for a particular period of time. Stop the process — stop eating —, and the actual reverts to mere potential.

Thus, Wealth is inherently *temporal*; not static, but *dynamic*.

quotes for comparison

Wealth is static.

Robert Heilbroner
(1919-2005)
quoted by James Galbraith in National Public Radio interview, "All Things Considered," January 11, 2005.

14

The popular conception of Wealth, assumed reflexively to be true by most economists and financial professionals alike, is that Wealth — inherently an individual notion, as opposed to measures of market activity, such as GDP — can be objectively measured in the abstract as a static quantity.

This prevailing view is, in short, that Wealth is *objective, abstract* and *static*.

This view manifests itself in acceptance of net worth as a measure of Wealth itself.

However, direct observation demonstrates that Wealth is in fact *subjective, contextual* and *dynamic*.

In the same way that bad or incomplete information undermines judgment in other contexts, using net worth as a surrogate for Wealth itself impairs the ability of well-intentioned individuals to make effective Wealth-related decisions.

Specifically, a net worth statement takes no account of the Capacity of the individual whose net worth is being measured.

Thus, the most important factor — the very *sine qua non* — of Wealth is missing altogether.

Meanwhile, the net worth statement takes no account of the individual's situation.

Thus, it ignores the fundamental difference between potential and actual Wealth, leaving out the contextual and temporal nature of Wealth altogether.

quotes for comparison

The Method I take to do this, is not yet very usual; for instead of using only comparative and superlative Words, and intellectual Arguments, I have taken the course. . . to express my self in Terms of Number, Weight, or Measure; to use only Arguments of Sense, and to consider only such Causes, as have visible Foundations in Nature.

William Petty
(1623-1687)
Political Arithmetick

15

Evaluating a person's height is easy, but evaluating a person's personality is not.

Yet we do not consider personality to be irrelevant or something we should ignore.

Evaluating a person's weight is easy, but evaluating a person's health is not.

Yet we do not consider health to be irrelevant or something we should ignore.

On the contrary, generally — and with good reason — we do *not* ignore important variables, even when they are hard to quantify.

Similarly, when we are calculating a result or predicting an outcome, ignoring major factors that go into that result or outcome virtually *assures* inaccuracy in our final analysis. Meanwhile, accounting for major variables — even through approximation — at least *allows* the possibility of accurate results.

Accordingly, if accuracy is a consideration at all in evaluating Wealth, responsible plutonomics requires that we not ignore the major factors that make up Wealth, even if those factors are hard to quantify.

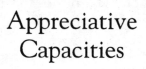

Appreciative
Capacities

Influential
Capacities

Part III
16

Capacity always implies a reference to at least one specific "capacity to _____."

Whatever goes in the blank — run, jump, speak — is a verb. A verb denotes a process, which means that Capacity inherently signifies potential to engage in a process.

The specific forms that Capacity takes can be usefully grouped into two categories: capacity to appreciate and capacity to influence.

When a capacity to appreciate is actualized, Appreciation occurs.

When a capacity to influence is actualized, Influence occurs.

quotes for comparison

First let us give what is necessary, next what is useful, and then what is pleasant, provided that they be lasting. We must begin with what is necessary, for those things which support life affect the mind very differently from those which adorn and improve it.

L. Annaeus Seneca
(circa 54 B.C. - circa 39 A.D.)
On Benefits

17

The category of appreciative capacities can be further divided into subcategories corresponding to the possible forms of Appreciation. Appreciation occurs on four basic levels:

— physical survival
— psychological survival
— comfort-pleasure
— connection

An alternate grouping system may be demonstrated to be superior at some later date.

Currently, however, these four levels appear to be best suited for the study and mastery of Wealth.

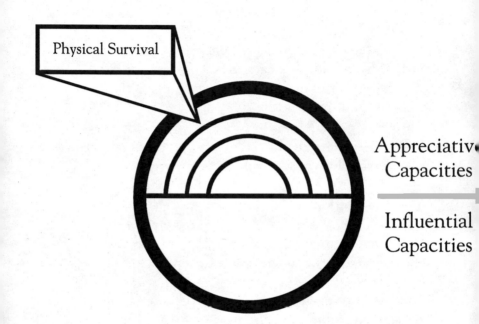

18

Physical survival is the most basic necessity of Wealth: dead people have no Wealth, even to those who believe that Wealth equals net worth.

In order for physical survival to occur, and therefore for Wealth to occur, myriad capacities to appreciate must be present, and actual Appreciation in a variety of forms must occur. Some specific appreciative capacities include:

— respiration
— digestion
— metabolism

The need for Appreciation at the physical survival level is what first drives each of us individually to learn the fundamental dynamics of Wealth. This need has driven individuals, families, tribes and nations to compete over land and other resources throughout history.

Appreciative capacity at the physical level is a primary reason why Wealth can differ dramatically from one individual to the next even when all objective external conditions remain constant. Age relentlessly erodes and eventually eliminates appreciative capacity, but hostile environmental conditions (e.g., smoke) or extended deprivations (e.g., starvation) can also impair physical appreciative capacity.

For instance, a prison camp survivor, upon liberation, may die moments after his first good meal in years: his body has lost the capacity to process certain food compounds such that what would otherwise be life-sustaining becomes deadly.

Medicine and biology are fields in which we study Capacity and Appreciation at the physical survival level.

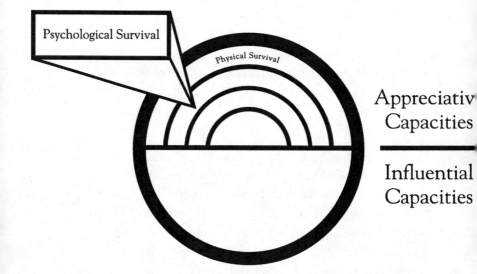

19

Psychological survival, typically involving invisible processes, is more difficult to study than physical survival. But destruction of the mind is hardly any less absolute than destruction of the body in its impact on Wealth: a brain-dead person, while still having net worth, has no Wealth.

For psychological survival to occur, and therefore for Wealth to occur, myriad capacities to appreciate must be present, and actual Appreciation must occur. In addition to at least the minimum amount of Appreciation at the physical survival level necessary to maintain the brain, Appreciation at the psychological survival level requires capacities such as:

— attention
— reason
— emotion
— empathy
— memory
— imagination
— communication
— identity

Short of that which literally kills us, no adversity cuts deeper into our Wealth than that which attacks at the psychological survival level. While a thief can steal our possessions and a stock market crash can undermine our financial security, diseases such as alzheimer's disease and schizophrenia steal our family, our friends, our jobs, our skills, even our own personal history and identity.

Psychology, medicine, biology and sociology are fields in which we examine these mental capacities and processes.

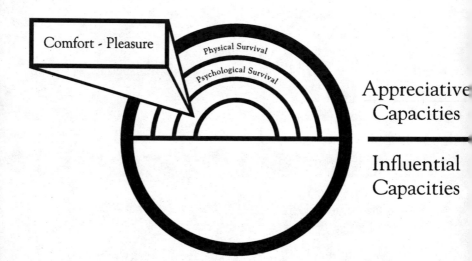

20

Comfort and pleasure involve matters of quality and quantity beyond that which is needed for mere survival. Appreciation at the comfort-pleasure level is not about simply eating, but eating *well*; not about simply sleeping, but sleeping *well*.

While the impact of comfort-pleasure on Wealth is not as dramatic as that of physical and psychological survival, Appreciation at the comfort-pleasure level is so desirable that, when survival is not in danger, we tend to pursue comfort and pleasure automatically, by default.

Moreover, Appreciation at the comfort-pleasure level can have a powerful, beneficial effect on capacities at other levels: comfort-pleasure can help rehabilitate an injured body or psyche and can fertilize the ground for Appreciation at the connection level.

Still, of the four levels of Appreciation, this level can be considered the most dispensable. In fact, self-denial of comfort-pleasure (e.g., vow of chastity) is an integral part of many spiritual practices, presumably to compel development of Capacity at the connection level.

While comfort-pleasure may be less often studied as an abstract, theoretical matter, items that evoke comfort-pleasure — fine cars, fine wine, fine jewelry — are almost universally considered to be symbols for Wealth. Practically speaking, comfort-pleasure is the *raison d'etre* of most consumer industries, from entertainment to fashion to travel.

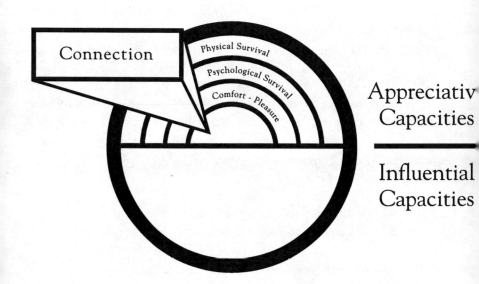

Connection

Physical Survival

Psychological Survival

Comfort - Pleasure

Appreciativ
Capacities

Influential
Capacities

21

The final level of Appreciation and appreciative Capacity is that of connection. Connection denotes two different but related concepts.

First, immersive connection signifies total immersion in an endeavor, the experience of being fully engrossed. Such immersion typically occurs on a short time frame, perhaps even a moment-to-moment basis. We often describe it as being "in the zone," "losing oneself," or "flow." It arises in all manner of activities, ranging from meditation to athletics, reading to music, building to sex. We often regard these periods of self-forgetfulness as peak moments in our lives.

Second, relational connection signifies bonding with those people and causes that endow our lives with meaning. This type of connection essentially reduces to relationships: our relationships with loved ones, with community, to social ideals, to principles of conscience, to religious and spiritual beliefs. It is experienced over a long time frame, indeed, across the span of an entire lifetime.

When we reflect upon a good day, we perceive a day of immersion. When we behold a good life, we recognize a life of relation.

There is significant interplay between these two forms of connection. Immersive experiences can help us to discover and tap more deeply into the meaning in our lives, and deep relational connection turns almost any activity into an opportunity for immersion.

Psychology, religion, philosophy and the arts are fields in which we undertake to explore and reveal immersive and relational connection.

quotes for comparison

The mind is its own place and in itself, can make a Heaven of Hell, a Hell of Heaven.

John Milton
(1608-1674)
Paradise Lost

22

As captured in these divisions, actual Appreciation generally can only occur when a particular form of Capacity meets a corresponding feature of Environment.

This general function is essentially analogous to that of an enzyme, representing a particular capacity to appreciate, encountering a substrate, representing a feature of Environment that can be appreciated.

But, in certain exceptions to this rule, the human mind is so wonderfully powerful that it appears able to create temporary, artificial conditions that produce actual Appreciation with no present reference to Environment.

Specifically, the twin powers of memory and imagination appear to be unique in that, through those powers, a human mind can temporarily conjure perceptions that have actual physical or psychological effects on the person — Appreciation —, even though these perceptions are not based in present external reality.

Granted, these powers are not literally autonomous in that memory can be treated simply as another effect of Appreciation that actually has occurred and imagination can be viewed as constructive recombination of such effects.

Nonetheless, since memory and imagination can be controlled — chosen — to a degree, do have demonstrable psychosomatic effects on humans, and can be tapped even absent any additional external stimulus, they do seem to have a genuine claim to being special "autonomous" forms of Capacity.

quotes for comparison

That man. . .has had a liberal education, who has been so trained in youth that his body is the ready servant of his will, and does with ease and pleasure all the work that. . .it is capable of; whose intellect is a clear, cold, logic engine, with all its parts of equal strength, and in smooth working order; ready, like a steam engine, to be turned to any kind of work. . .whose mind is stored with a knowledge of the great and fundamental truths of Nature and of the laws of her operations; one who, no stunted ascetic, is full of life and fire, but whose passions are trained to come to heel by a vigorous will, the servant of a tender conscience; who has learned to love all beauty, whether of Nature or of art, to hate all vileness, and to respect others as himself.

Thomas Henry Huxley
(1825-1895)
Lay Sermons, Addresses and Reviews

23

These, therefore, are the four subcategories or levels into which the capacity to appreciate and Appreciation itself can be divided: physical survival, psychological survival, comfort-pleasure and connection.

When Environment affects the person whose Wealth is being considered, Appreciation occurs, and such Appreciation can be characterized as falling into one or more of these subcategories.

quotes for comparison

What I am and can do is, therefore, not at all determined by my individuality. I am ugly, but I can buy the most beautiful woman for myself. Consequently, I am not ugly, for the effect of ugliness, its power to repel, is annulled by money. As an individual I am lame, but money provides me with twenty-four legs. Therefore, I am not lame. I am a detestable, dishonourable, unscrupulous and stupid man, but money is honoured and so also is its possessor. Money is the highest good, and so its possessor is good. Besides, money saves me the trouble of being dishonest; therefore, I am presumed honest. I am stupid, but since money is the real mind of all things, how should its possessor be stupid? Moreover, he can buy talented people for himself, and is not he who has power over the talented more talented than they?

Karl Marx
(1818-1883)
Economical and Philosophical Manuscripts

Part IV
24

Capacity to influence can likewise be divided into subcategories corresponding to the types of Influence itself.

These are:

— physical influence
— social influence
— mental influence

This grouping scheme, being based on bright-line distinctions, enables discussion of Influence at a level of generality that is unavailable under current theories of Wealth.

It stands in stark contrast to the modern trend in economics, which is to seek to overcome basic theoretical inadequacies through sheer volume of "exceptions to the rule," trusting in complexity and specificity over simplicity and generality, generating a steady stream of qualifications, disclaimers and add-ons.

However, as criticality theorists point out, analysis of each part of a system may be inadequate to predict the behavior of a system as a whole.

Thus, for those who wish to consider whole systems rather than individual parts, a robust, cohesive and flexible general theory serves better than a mosaic of disjointed — if not contradictory — economic and financial microtheses.

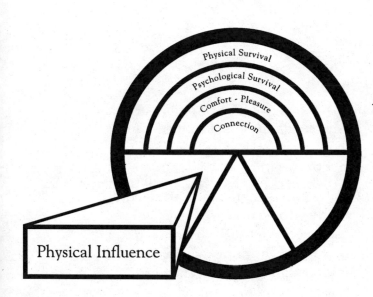

25

J ust as the most basic Appreciation is physical, the most basic Influence is also physical.

Whenever we pick up a pen or a stone, whenever we harvest crops or dam a river, whenever we run around a track or move to another city, we are exerting Influence on a physical level. Any action taken that directly changes either Environment or our physical relationship to Environment is physical influence.

Physical influence can be exerted equally upon animate creatures and inanimate objects, taking forms such as:

— walking, running, jumping
— manipulating (a pen, a guitar, a screwdriver)
— gesturing, signalling

Physical influence is the most reliable type of Influence. Particularly in times of disaster or anarchy, as in the case of a fire or a riot — when social influence becomes largely irrelevant —, we are reminded of the supremacy of physical influence. These reminders can be bitter: the world was appalled to learn that, in the aftermath of a recent hurricane and flood, basic laws and rights (social influence) were summarily ignored by residents of a major modern city, who turned instead to the laws of the jungle, namely, physical influence. Such news surprises us to the degree to which we have lost touch with the basics.

The hard sciences and engineering are areas of study of physical influence over objects. Military and police sciences and martial arts are areas of study of physical influence over humans.

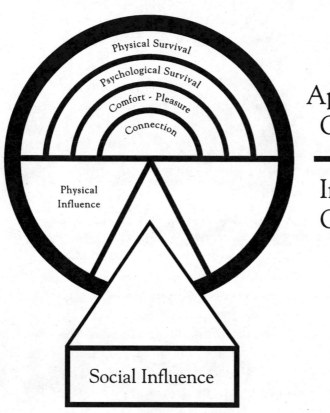

Physical Survival

Psychological Survival

Comfort - Pleasure

Connection

Physical
Influence

Social Influence

Appreciative
Capacities

Influential
Capacities

26

Unlike physical influence, social influence can only be exerted on living, sentient creatures.

All legal rights, such as property and citizenship, are social influence.

Money is social influence.

All interpersonal bonds with friends and family are social influence.

Reputation and status are social influence.

Also unlike physical influence, social influence is entirely dependent upon the perception of other living beings. For example, money and law have little or no effect on people who do not recognize the currency or law at issue. Thus, social influence obeys rules that are constantly changing and extremely sensitive to context and individual eccentricities.

While social influence requires awareness on the part of the party being influenced, much of social influence can and does occur without any effort or even present awareness on the part of the individual wielding the Influence. In fact, a person can be comatose and still wield tremendous social influence.

Politics, economics, finance, business, marketing, law, ethics, fashion and etiquette are fields directed toward the study or exertion of social influence.

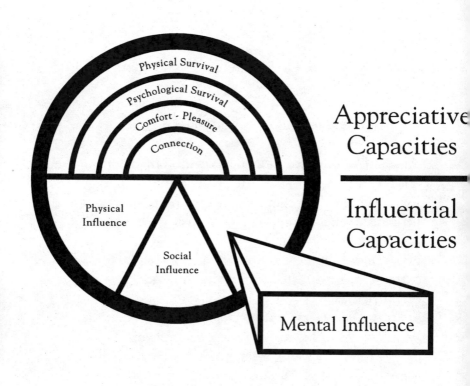

27

Mental influence denotes any intentional act of *omission* rather than *commission*.

If we choose to save a drowning person, this act of commission is clearly physical influence.

But when we choose *not* to save such a person, not to act at all, we have, in a sense, influenced Environment to the degree that what actually happens differs from what would have happened if we had intervened.

This act of omission, made by conscious, voluntary choice, is called mental influence.

Perhaps mental influence is best understood as Influence exerted by a person neither physically nor socially, nor on any part of Environment directly, but rather on himself or herself; it is a sort of "autonomous" Influence, analogous in this respect to memory and imagination as forms of Appreciation.

In many cases, one person's social influence is manifested in another's mental influence. For instance, if we choose not to save the drowning person because he or she is an enemy soldier in time of war, that person's social influence — citizenship and military status — is manifested in our decision not to act — mental influence.

Law often works as a combination of one person's mental influence and another's social influence: one person chooses not to cross over a piece of land (mental influence) because he or she knows another person owns the land (social influence).

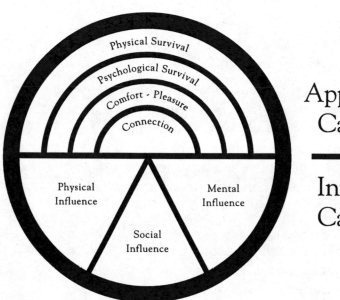

Physical Survival

Psychological Survival

Comfort - Pleasure

Connection

Physical Influence

Mental Influence

Social Influence

Appreciative
Capacities

Influential
Capacities

28

These, therefore, are the three basic groupings of Influence and the capacity to influence: physical, social and mental influence.

When a person directly or indirectly affects Environment or his or her relationship to Environment, Influence occurs, and such Influence can be characterized as falling into one of these subcategories.

Just as Appreciation and Influence often occur simultaneously and arise out of the same event, occurrences of Influence need not be treated as falling in only one subcategory. For instance, when a person speaks, he or she exerts physical influence by making a physical sound and, provided that a second person is present to hear and interpret (i.e., appreciate) what is being said, also exerts social influence.

Some key distinctions between the types of Influence should be noted: being strictly dependent upon the perception of others, social influence can be exerted by an individual through communication, persuasion, attraction, intimidation or mere bluff. Thus, in the area of social influence, manipulating appearances can have a direct impact on Wealth.

Similarly, being strictly dependent upon the subjective perception of the individual whose Wealth is at issue, mental influence puts no premium on truth. Myths, false beliefs, and bad information carry as much weight in the mind of an individual as they would if they were valid. Thus, in the area of mental influence, managing one's own thoughts and memories bears directly upon Wealth.

By contrast, physical influence is perception-independent. Falsehoods are irrelevant.

quotes for comparison

Goods are produced and consumed as a means to the fuller unfolding of human life; and their utility consists, in the first instance, in their efficiency as means to this end. The end is, in the first instance, the fullness of life of the individual, taken in absolute terms.

Thorstein Veblen
(1857-1929)
The Theory of the Leisure Class

Part V
29

Just as Capacity can be divided into categories, so Environment can be divided.

Features of Environment can be usefully grouped into these divisions:

— appreciables, meaning phenomena that can be appreciated by a person whose Wealth is being considered

— influenceables, meaning phenomena that can be influenced by the person

— inaccessibles, meaning phenomena that can neither be influenced nor appreciated

The concept of an appreciable readily accommodates the many different classes of "goods" identified in economics as well as numerous phenomena that are fully relevant to Wealth but largely lost in economics, e.g., an item that has extreme sentimental value to a particular individual but is basically worthless to anyone else.

Just as Appreciation itself can be either beneficial or detrimental, the appreciables group also fully encompasses potentially harmful features of Environment — from viruses to verbal threats —, "bads" that are only addressed indirectly in economics (through goods and services used to avoid or counteract these bads), if addressed at all.

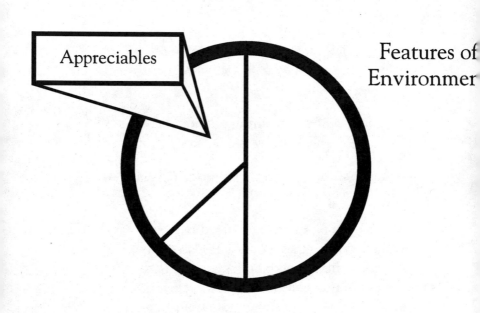

30

Appreciables include:
- food, water, medicine
- land
- information, entertainment
- anything beautiful, pleasing or comfortable
- friends, lovers and allies

Appreciables are generally a necessary ingredient of Appreciation, and Appreciation is necessary to survival. Thus, no part of Environment attracts more attention than appreciables, and the more readily and commonly appreciable something is, the more attention it attracts.

Scarcity of some beneficial appreciables gave rise to the science of economics, necessitates competition between individuals and between nations, and serves as a primary mechanism in natural selection.

Non-scarcity of appreciables — increasingly common in an age of infinitely replicable digital goods, such as downloadable music files — has in turn wrought significant changes in the nature of business and cast doubt on the viability of some long-standing economic notions, once prompting temporary declaration of a "new economy."

Plutonomic theory, by contrast, retains its explanatory and predictive viability regardless of whether contextual conditions of scarcity or non-scarcity predominate; capitalism, socialism or communism prevails; or democracy, monarchy, theocracy or anarchy reigns.

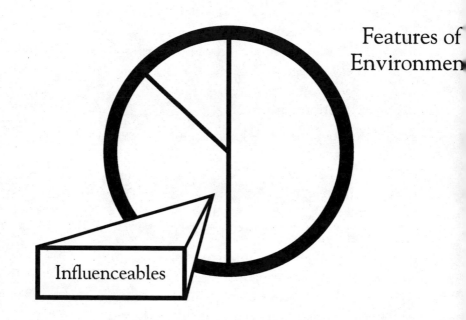

Features of
Environmen

Influenceables

31

While beneficial appreciables may be the object of our immediate desire, Influence is often the best way to attain access to appreciables, and influenceables are generally necessary to Influence. Influenceables are, therefore, primarily a means to an end. Influenceables include:

— anything that can be legally owned or physically affected, such as land, cars and money
— anyone who can be socially, culturally or personally affected

While, at any given time, that which is appreciable is severely limited by capacity limits — a stomach can only hold so much food —, such limitations oftentimes do not apply to social influence. Our capacity to own money and property, for instance, is unlimited and not subject to marginal diminution: one can own a million dollars as completely as one can own ten dollars.

Since such forms of social influence can be accumulated infinitely, the desire for influenceables can become for some a sort of endless quest, such that sheer ownership takes on an Appreciation role, even if the things owned cannot be appreciated in and of themselves.

On a more practical level, massive accumulation of certain influenceables can mask or compensate for a lack of other forms of Influence: money may be used to distract attention from a lack of beauty or, through marketing, philanthropy, conspicuous consumption or outright bribery, converted into reputation or favor.

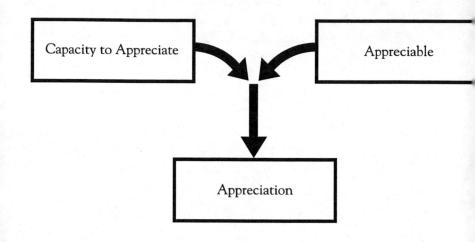

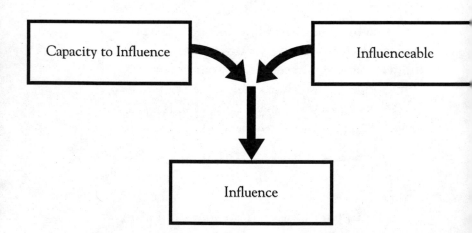

32

Many of the most important appreciables are also influenceables.

A glass of wine can be picked up — influenced — and then imbibed and digested — appreciated.

A lover can be influenced by one's own appearance and appreciated as an instance of beauty.

While in such cases the processes of Appreciation and Influence are occurring simultaneously, the fundamentally distinct nature of these two processes does not change.

Thus, the glass of wine or the lover can be viewed from both perspectives: the ways in which this feature of Environment is appreciable and the ways in which it is influenceable.

The overlap between these two categories does not always occur, however: one cannot influence the events of a thousand years ago, but can appreciate them; one cannot appreciate events that will happen a thousand years from now, but can influence them.

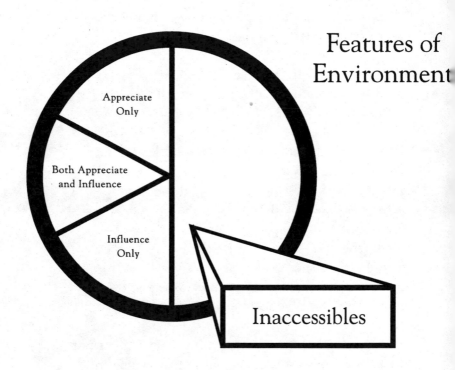

Features of Environment

Appreciate Only

Both Appreciate and Influence

Influence Only

Inaccessibles

33

The vast majority — just short of 100% — of environmental features fall into the final category, that of inaccessibles.

Most of the universe is unknown and wholly impervious to any given human being.

Such features have no impact on the Wealth of the person being considered. However, that which is inaccessible at one point in time can become appreciable or influenceable or both at another point in time.

New people and places and things, once fully irrelevant, come into our lives, affect us and are affected by us.

Others depart, never to return, becoming inaccessible except with respect to any lingering or delayed effects.

Thus, these distinctions between features of Environment are, like Wealth itself, contextual and dynamic.

34

These, therefore, are the three categories into which Environment, for the purposes of plutonomic analysis, may be divided: appreciables, influenceables and inaccessibles.

The first two categories often overlap, and the final category changes significantly over time.

Fundamental Dynamic of Wealth

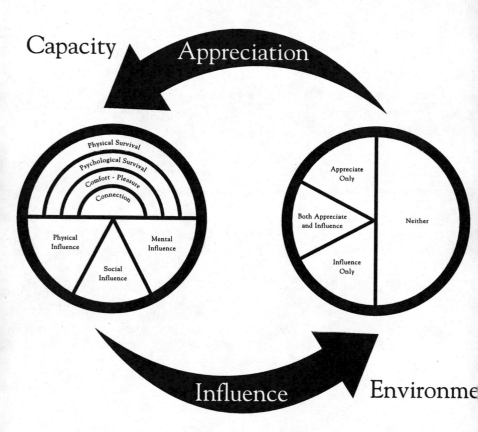

Capacity

Appreciation

Physical Survival

Psychological Survival

Comfort - Pleasure

Connection

Physical Influence

Mental Influence

Social Influence

Appreciate Only

Both Appreciate and Influence

Neither

Influence Only

Influence

Environme

Part VI

35

Plutonomic analysis contemplates the in-here, Capacity, and the out-there, Environment, as well as the two processes whereby in-here and out-there interact: Appreciation, being the effect of Environment on Capacity, and Influence, the effect of Capacity on Environment.

This analysis is further elaborated in delineating four basic levels of Appreciation and three basic types of Influence.

Upon this *fundamental dynamic of wealth*, the ways in which the four factors of Wealth combine to form Wealth can be examined.

quotes for comparison

"And what if I had been accused of robbing a dead man, Gaffer?"

"You COULDN'T do it."

"Couldn't you, Gaffer?"

"No. Has a dead man any use for money? Is it possible for a dead man to have money? What world does a dead man belong to? 'Tother world. What world does money belong to? This world. How can money be a corpse's? Can a corpse own it, want it, spend it, claim it, miss it?"

Charles Dickens
(1812-1870)
Our Mutual Friend

36

As demonstrated, Wealth is subjective, dynamic and contextual. Like its factors Appreciation and Influence, Wealth "occurs" rather than "is." It is a process.

Assigning a value to a process can be misleading: processes are just not susceptible to simple quantification in the way that pounds or prices are, especially processes that are multifaceted and highly variable, like Wealth.

But, as rational beings, we also want measurements of some kind in order to make informed decisions.

Toward the goal of quantifying Wealth so as to assist in Wealth-related decisions and comparisons, representation of Wealth in the form of an — albeit imperfect — equation can be undertaken.

quotes for comparison

The Value, or WORTH of a man, is as of all other things, his Price. . . so much as would be given for the use of his Power: and therefore is not absolute; but a thing dependant on the need and judgement of another.   An able conductor of Souldiers, is of great Price in time of War present, or imminent; but in Peace not so. . . . And as in other things, so in men, not the seller, but the buyer determines the Price. For let a man (as most men do,) rate themselves as the highest Value they can; yet their true Value is no more than it is esteemed by others.

Thomas Hobbes
(1588-1679)
Leviathan

37

To see Wealth occurring and to undertake to measure Wealth, we must observe Wealth over a period of time, just as we would observe any other process, such as swimming or cooking.

While future developments in plutonomics will likely produce superior insights, at least two basic approaches to this observation can currently be taken.

First, we can observe Wealth as a short-term event, much as we might observe a swimmer in a particular race.

Second, we can observe Wealth over a long-term span, much as we might observe a swimmer's entire swimming career.

How we characterize Wealth and the factors of Wealth differs according to whether a short-term or long-term assessment is being made.

Short-term evaluations assist in making effective Wealth decisions for a particular set of fixed circumstances, and long-term evaluations assist in making effective Wealth decisions on a life-planning level.

quotes for comparison

To a person considered by himself, the value of a pleasure or pain considered by itself, will be greater or less, according to the four following circumstances:

Its intensity.
Its duration.
Its certainty or uncertainty.
Its propinquity or remoteness.

Jeremy Bentham
(1748-1832)
An Introduction to the Principles of Morals and Legislation

38

When performing a short-term evaluation for the purposes of making a good Wealth decision under fixed circumstances, use of a prospective equation may be preferable. The prospective equation is:

Wealth is the likelihood that an individual will actually enjoy, from the moment of measurement on, the Appreciation and Influence he or she would choose to enjoy if put to the choice.

Since Appreciation and Influence are inherently processes, and since these processes typically occur only when corresponding Capacity and Environment coincide, this equation accommodates all four factors as well as the subjective, dynamic and contextual nature of Wealth.

By treating Wealth as a matter of likelihood, this equation readily captures Wealth differences which we intuitively grasp yet cannot represent in net worth form. For instance, consider two millionaires: one is a healthy 25 year-old; the other is an 85 year-old cancer patient. Most of us have an unequivocal sense of which of these two *dramatis personae* has greater Wealth, yet their respective net worth may be identical.

The reason for our intuitive grasp of the situation is made explicit in the prospective equation: the likelihood of the one actually having Influence and Appreciation *occur* is much greater than that of the other. For one, Wealth will likely occur in the future, and it may occur for an extended period of time. For the other, the prospects for Wealth are slim and brief, regardless of how much money sits idly in a bank account somewhere.

Accuracy
> The degree to which a measurement conforms to the true value of the thing being measured; veracity.

Precision
> The degree to which a group of measurements conform to each other; reproducibility.

Precision Bias
> The tendency to believe that greater precision implies greater accuracy; the tendency to afford more credence or assign more weight to that which can be easily quantified than to that which defies quantification.

39

One virtue of the prospective equation is that it is robust.

Even under highly unusual circumstances, such as natural catastrophe or political anarchy, this equation comports with reality in a way that market-based definitions do not. It is not rendered meaningless or impotent under "market failure" conditions, where economics- and finance-based theories break down or fall silent: no one on a sinking ship will trade his or her seat on a lifeboat for money, yet physical coercion remains — rightly or wrongly — a viable means of obtaining a seat.

Meanwhile, this equation does not ignore the *sine qua non* of Wealth, Capacity, or pretend that every person of every age has identical Capacity.

It does not ignore the risk that potential will never become actual.

It does not pretend that the situation of living, changing beings moving through time is static.

In short, what the foregoing equation may sacrifice in *precision*, relative to the common view, it gains in *accuracy* and *reliability*.

As a value judgment, plutonomic analysis posits that, if only one of the two is possible, accuracy is to be preferred over precision.

quotes for comparison

For a life without life's joys I count a living death. You'll tell me he has ample store of wealth, the pomp and circumstance of kings; but if these give no pleasure, all the rest I count the shadow of a shade, nor would I weigh his wealth and power 'gainst a dram of joy.

Sophocles
(circa 496 B.C.-406 B.C.)
Antigone

40

When performing a long-term evaluation of Wealth, one geared toward effective decision-making on a life-planning level, we may prefer to apply a retrospective equation of Wealth. The retrospective equation is:

Wealth is the degree of correlation between the actual Appreciation and Influence enjoyed by an individual during a measured time span and the Appreciation and Influence he or she would have chosen to have enjoyed during that span if put to the choice.

The key difference in the retrospective equation vis-a-vis the prospective equation is that, in the retrospective equation, correlation of actual and ideal replaces likelihood of realizing potential.

Because a retrospective evaluation of how events actually transpired offers more certainty than a prospective estimation of future events, the retrospective equation may serve better as a source for extracting general principles, making it more useful for long-term planning.

Once we have applied the retrospective equation of Wealth, we attempt to analyze the causes for discrepancy between actual and ideal, extract principles, and then implement strategies based on these principles.

quotes for comparison

The cost of a thing is the amount of what I will call life which is required to be exchanged for it, immediately or in the long run.

> Henry David Thoreau
> (1817-1862)
> *Walden*

Wealth is the ability to fully experience life.

> Thoreau
> attributed

41

Like the prospective equation, the retrospective equation comports with reality in a way that market-only definitions do not.

For instance, when we compare the Wealth of a prisoner to that of a free person, even if these two individuals have indistinguishable net worth statements, observation of their respective lives over a certain period of time typically indicates that the free person enjoys significantly higher Wealth than the prisoner, as is readily conveyed through plutonomic analysis: the prisoner is, in most cases, barred from Appreciation (e.g., going out to a concert) and Influence (e.g., voting) that he or she would otherwise be enjoying and would prefer to enjoy.

But these facts escape any representation in a net worth analysis or market-based surrogate for Wealth, which would lead us to believe that the prisoner and the free person had identical Wealth.

quotes for comparison

It is not the possessor of many things whom you will rightly call happy. The name of the happy man is claimed more justly by him who has learnt the art whereby to use what the gods give.

Horace
(65-8 B.C.)
Odes

42

A different kind of example is that of a child in a wealthy family who owns virtually nothing in his or her own right and therefore has negligible net worth. Yet the child has access to multiple beautiful homes, the finest food and health care, art and social events, and numerous other luxuries.

The Wealth of such children — far in excess of that of many people with greater net worth — is readily expressed in the plutonomic equations, notably, through their Influence on *people* who in turn have great Influence in the form of property rights.

Yet, using net worth or market-based analyses, one would conclude that such individuals had negligible Wealth.

Many positions of status also enable immense Wealth without any significant net worth. The Pope is probably the ultimate embodiment of this phenomenon: while he may own next to nothing, he enjoys some of the most opulent settings known to the human race and wields global Influence that is rivaled in scope by few.

quotes for comparison

Money is human happiness in abstract; so that a man who is no longer capable of enjoying it in concrete gives up his whole heart to it.

Arthur Schopenhauer
(1788-1860)
Essays of Schopenhauer

43

Net worth remains an excellent means of quantifying a subset of social influence, namely, property rights, at a particular point in time.

The problem with net worth simply arises when we mistake net worth to be a reliable indicator of Wealth itself.

A brain-dead accident victim can have a high net worth, and a healthy, happy, wealthy prince can have a low net worth — or even no or negative net worth.

Thus, while not insignificant, the net worth statement is simply inadequate to serve as a representative or meaningfully complete depiction of individual Wealth itself.

Book II

Mastering Wealth

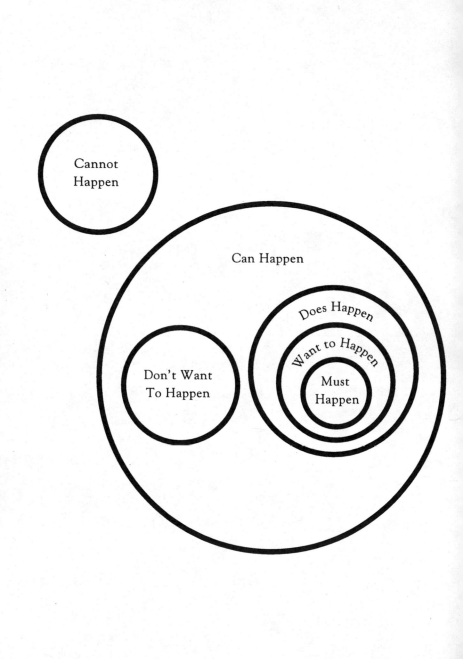

Part VII
44

Wealth happens.

To master Wealth is to excel at enabling Wealth to happen.

Specifically, mastery of Wealth is excellence at causing or allowing two sets of processes, those which *must* occur and those which one *wants* to occur, to fall within a third set, that which *does* occur. The day that a process in the must-occur set falls outside of the does-occur set, life itself ends, and so, of course, does Wealth.

Knowing these musts and wants is often crucial to causing or allowing them to occur.

Most musts and wants pertain to Capacity, particularly the capacities to appreciate, and mastery of Wealth begins with Capacity accordingly.

quotes for comparison

Thus it is clear that household management attends more to men than to the acquisition of inanimate things, and to human excellence more than to the excellence of property.

Aristotle
(384-322 B.C.)
Politics

45

Regarding Capacity, several general observations can be made.

Capacity is unique to and essential to living creatures. Regardless of one's philosophical or religious position, Capacity can be characterized as that which departs a body at death.

Only Capacity begets Capacity. A person is endowed with Capacity only by living parents, and no instance of spontaneous generation has been shown to contravene this rule.

Almost all Capacity is bestowed on a person at the outset of life. After life begins, expansion in Capacity occurs very slowly and requires a great investment of resources, whereas reduction or elimination of Capacity can occur instantaneously and easily.

quotes for comparison

I fully subscribe to the judgment of those writers who maintain that, of all the differences between man and the lower animals, the moral sense or conscience is by far the most important. . . . It is the most noble of all the attributes of man.

Charles Darwin
(1809-1882)
The Descent of Man

46

Expanding Capacity refers to growth, both physical and mental, of a person.

Such growth includes:

— becoming physically stronger and larger
— maturation, e.g., becoming able to reproduce
— acquiring skills, such as walking, speech and computation
— developing self-awareness, consciousness
— developing spiritual and emotional abilities, such as empathy and conscience

These and countless similar instances of growth can only be achieved through years of eating, sleeping, exercise, rehearsal, practice, education, socialization, reflection and an otherwise enormous investment of time, effort and other resources.

There is truly no shortcut from human infancy to adulthood.

quotes for comparison

"My name is Ozymandias, king of kings:
Look on my works, ye mighty, and despair!"
Nothing beside remains: round the decay
Of that colossal wreck, boundless and bare,
The lone and level sands stretch far away.

Percy Bysshe Shelley
(1792-1822)
"Ozymandias"

47

Meanwhile, all Capacity one gains at birth and all that one adds during life can be obliterated in an instant.

An automobile accident, a fall, an intentional act of violence, an infectious disease — any of these hostile stimuli can undo years of growth or bring an end to life itself.

The circumstances giving rise to such events are not hard to create. In fact, almost any time we get in a car or a plane, we are putting our entire Capacity at stake.

Once Capacity has been reduced, recovery can take years — if the lost Capacity can even be regained at all.

quotes for comparison

Economics: The study of the way in which mankind organises itself to tackle the basic problem of scarcity. All societies have more wants than resources (the factors of production), so that a system must be devised to allocate these resources between competing ends.

The MIT Dictionary of Modern Economics, Fourth Ed.
(1992)
Edited by David W. Pearce
MIT Press

48

Capacity cannot be transferred.

One person cannot buy, borrow or steal another person's running skills or eyesight or aptitude for math.

Granted, medical technology has made this once-absolute rule blurry around the edges, since certain transplant procedures do amount to a transfer of Capacity.

However, in the vast majority of contexts, Capacity remains completely non-transferable.

This characteristic partly explains why economics, which by design deals with things that are allocable, is of so little value in analyzing Wealth: the bulk of Wealth is non-transferable, non-allocable.

quotes for comparison

Upon the subject of education, not presuming to dictate any plan or system respecting it, I can only say that I view it as the most important subject which we as a people can be engaged in.

Abraham Lincoln
(1809-1865)
Public address, Sangamo County, March 9, 1832

49

Despite its non-transferability, Capacity generally *can* and *can only* be imparted.

At birth, our parents do not transfer their Capacity to us, but they do impart Capacity to us, and they do so without losing their own Capacity.

Skills, such as language and any number of basic behaviors, are also imparted to us by others without dimunition of their own skills.

Thus, unlike dollars or diamonds or drugs, Capacity can be given and kept at the same time, as a flame is passed from one candle to another.

Capacity is, in short, not a zero-sum concept but is instead jatallic.

That the central feature of Wealth is jatallic may partly explain why social reformers throughout the ages have often looked first to education. By facilitating development of Capacity in the general population, education permits the Wealth of an entire group of people to be increased without a corresponding loss of Wealth to others.

The jatallic nature of Capacity may also partly explain why societies that protect dissemination of information (e.g., through free speech rights) and reward disclosure of knowledge (e.g., through patent rights) have prospered, while those that suppress sharing of information have tended to decline.

quotes for comparison

The universe is sacred. You cannot improve it. If you try to change it, you will ruin it. If you try to hold it, you will lose it.

Lao Tzu
(circa 500 B.C.)
Tao Te Ching

50

Capacity generally functions as a system, holistically, synergistically.

Most forms of Capacity cannot be separated from the remaining forms without being destroyed, and harm to one form of Capacity often reverberates harmfully throughout many other forms.

Nowhere is this trait more apparent than in the human body itself, wherein harm to one organ harms, if not destroys, the rest.

This synergism further underscores the delicate nature of Capacity. Small losses in Capacity can open the door to much larger ones.

Such interdependence also appears in societies. When the Capacity of certain individuals is harmed or stunted through unjust laws, ostracism, witch-hunting, and book- and cross-burning, additional negative effects on Wealth ripple throughout the culture: knowledge, wisdom and insight that would have otherwise been shared get lost, taken to the grave by those who are oppressed.

quotes for comparison

If any thing is sacred, the human body is sacred.

Walt Whitman
(1819-1892)
Leaves of Grass

51

These characteristics of Capacity — non-transferability, jatallic passing, holistic functioning, difficult expansion, easy destruction — give rise to a first Wealth goal, which can be stated as an imperative:

Capacity must be preserved.

In particular, and above all else, preservation of the physical apparatus given to us at birth — brain, heart, lungs, eyes, ears, hands and the rest — and all the associated intellectual, emotional and motor skills is the single most important must in the mastery of Wealth.

Risks to Capacity, accordingly, must be considered uniquely serious.

52

The preceding imperative can be elaborated in at least two specific Wealth maxims:

The primary justification for risking Capacity is that a greater risk to Capacity is thereby avoided.

The primary justification for sacrificing Capacity is that a greater loss of Capacity is thereby avoided.

Generally, under these maxims, Influence or Appreciation alone do not suffice to justify risk or sacrifice of Capacity. However, Appreciation is necessary to preservation of Capacity, and Influence is often the only means of avoiding a loss of Capacity.

One area of inquiry left open is how best to characterize risks or sacrifices of Capacity by one individual on behalf of another. This topic becomes more important the more bonded with and interdependent upon others a person becomes. Especially in cases where the connection in our lives depends upon specific individuals, namely, our loved ones, many of us would without hesitation undertake almost unlimited risks on their behalf.

Perhaps this reality implies that, while connection alone may not be sufficient for Wealth, it is intuitively recognized as necessary to Wealth — or simply trumps the notion of Wealth altogether.

Whatever the case, these two maxims may underlie many of our moral and ethical rules. For instance, physically harming someone else is unjustifiable unless a greater or at least similar harm is thereby averted, as in a case of self-defense.

quotes for comparison

Consider these people, then, their way of life, their habits, their manners, the very tones of their voice; look at them attentively; observe the literature they read, the things which give them pleasure, the words which come forth out of their mouths, the thoughts which make the furniture of their minds; would any amount of wealth be worth having with the condition that one was to become just like these people by having it?

Matthew Arnold
(1822-1888)
Culture and Anarchy

53

The first wealth imperative in its most basic form is expressly limited to preserving Capacity. Expanding Capacity may not always be necessary to Wealth or even possible.

That being said, however, expanding or adjusting Capacity is often a powerful method of *increasing* Wealth, and a certain amount of Capacity cultivation is indeed necessary for enjoyment of *high* Wealth.

For instance, the potential Wealth represented in a book is lost on one who has not the capacity to read.

Meanwhile, a handful of individual forms of Capacity make us vulnerable to external dangers: an allergy, for example. In the case of such vulnerabilities, a reduction of Capacity is actually useful.

Thus, instead of the basic phrasing, a more complex imperative may be used:

Capacity must generally be preserved, and, where possible, should be optimized.

This rule accommodates the context-dependent desirability of Capacity cultivation or reduction.

quotes for comparison

After the means of subsistence are assured, the next in strength of the personal wants of human beings is liberty; and (unlike the physical wants, which as civilization advances become more moderate and more amenable to control) it increases instead of diminishing in intensity, as the intelligence and the moral faculties are more developed.

John Stuart Mill
(1806-1873)
Principles of Political Economy

Part VIII
54

$\mathbb{D}$iscussing Wealth in terms of means and ends can be somewhat misleading, for, within the processes that make up Wealth, both means-like and ends-like functions can be happening simultaneously.

Nonetheless, conceptually it is useful to view these processes through a means lens so that we can begin learning how not only to understand but also to affect our Wealth.

The effectiveness of a Wealth means is determined by how well that means causes or allows the first two sets, *musts* and *wants*, to fall into the third set, what actually *does* occur.

Empirically, it appears that, while not the only, the single most powerful means of preserving and enhancing Capacity, avoiding detrimental Appreciation, and facilitating beneficial Appreciation can be summarized in one word.

Choice.

quotes for comparison

This freedom from absolute, arbitrary power, is so necessary to, and closely joined with a man's preservation, that he cannot part with it, but by what forfeits his preservation and life together.

John Locke
(1632-1704)
The Second Treatise of Government

55

Consider the power of choice: even if someone has full capacity to eat and digest and has readily accessible food — in short, has all the necessary ingredients for beneficial Appreciation that would serve to preserve Capacity — he or she may still choose not to eat. Most other forms of beneficial Appreciation can also be willfully rejected.

In other words, choice can negate or embrace an entire universe of potential Wealth. In the extreme, choice — manifested in suicide — can end Wealth and life itself.

Moreover, every time we choose an action, or inaction, we are inherently choosing not to pursue a thousand other actions. Each such action, undertaken or forgone, has a Wealth impact.

Things that are immutable, inevitable or impossible, i.e., beyond choice, are not part of mastery, and it is beyond the scope of plutonomics to contemplate the philosophical or religious implications of choice and free will. Rather, for the purposes of the study and mastery of Wealth, we simply postulate that each human being has certain latitude in the choices he or she can make.

Given the unequalled power of choice, the ability to make effective Wealth decisions — choices that cause or allow Wealth to happen — is essential to mastery of Wealth. The rest is up to fate, fortune or divine will.

By extension, the individual who seeks Wealth should seek to become an excellent chooser, to have excellent decision-making skills, to choose better.

quotes for comparison

Those who won our independence believed that the final end of the state was to make men free to develop their faculties. . . . They valued liberty both as an end and as a means. They believed liberty to be the secret of happiness and courage to be the secret of liberty. . . . that the greatest menace to freedom is an inert people.

Louis Brandeis
(1856-1941)
Whitney v. California (concurring)

56

$\mathbb{B}$ecause that which restricts choice impairs our most potent means to Wealth, a second Wealth imperative arises:

The power to choose must be enabled, protected and exercised.

However, unlike most threats to Capacity, threats to choice can come not only from outside but also from within. Specifically, not *knowing* or *understanding* one's options can be as bad as not *having* any options.

In other words, choice is a much broader and more complex notion than simply having "choices" or options from which to choose. Choice presupposes an entire superstructure of multiple forms of Capacity — reason, imagination — as well as actual information.

Moreover, simply having the power to choose is not full enablement of choice. If a person chooses detrimental options — whether out of ignorance or weakness of will —, he or she would have been better off to have been without these options.

The prospects and pitfalls surrounding choice send a clear message: learning and enlightenment — through contemplation, study, education, experience — are essential to enabling and protecting choice, and willingness to act in accordance with this learning is essential to the effective exercise of choice.

Learning and willingness are the heart of Wealth mastery.

quotes for comparison

To every thing there is a season, and a time to every purpose under the heaven. A time to be born, and a time to die; a time to plant, and a time to pluck up that which is planted. A time to kill, and a time to heal; a time to break down, and a time to build up. A time to weep, and a time to laugh; a time to mourn, and a time to dance. A time to cast away stones, and a time to gather stones together; a time to embrace, and a time to refrain from embracing. A time to get, and a time to lose; a time to keep, and a time to cast away. A time to rend, and a time to sew; a time to keep silence, and a time to speak. A time to love, and a time to hate; a time of war, and a time of peace.

Ecclesiastes (circa 250 B.C.)

57

Given the impossibility of addressing all possible life situations, choice can best be characterized as the confluence of a set of priorities and a decision aimed to serve those priorities. The decision is an act or omission selected as a vehicle for such service.

What to choose is, like Wealth itself, inherently contextual. There is no universal template for mastery of Wealth.

However, we can be guided in our exercise of choice by principles that follow from our direct observations of the manifold of Wealth.

Perceiving how priorities can best be served in a given situation or over the course of a lifetime is a boundless art form, mastery of Wealth a lifelong journey.

quotes for comparison

"Money," they say, "is the symbol of duty, it is the sacrament of having done for mankind that which mankind wanted. Mankind may not be a very good judge, but there is no better." This used to shock me at first, when I remembered that it had been said on high authority that they who have riches shall enter hardly into the kingdom of heaven; but the influence of Erewhon had made me begin to see things in a new light, and I could not help thinking that they who have not riches shall enter more hardly still.

People oppose money to culture, and imply that if a man has spent his time in making money he will not be cultivated — fallacy of fallacies! As though there could be a greater aid to culture than the having earned an honourable independence, and as though any amount of culture will do much for the man who is penniless, except make him feel his position more deeply. . . . It has been said that the love of money is the root of all evil. The want of money is so quite as truly.

Samuel Butler
(1835-1902)
Erewhon

Part IX
58

There are two basic modes in which Wealth-related choices are implemented.

We can either choose (i) to wield Influence, hoping to alter Environment or our relationship to it so as to suit our existing Capacity, or (ii) to alter our Capacity so as as to be more suitable for our present or expected Environment. Most choices involve both modes to some degree.

The former mode, that of asserting control over Environment, is ground that has been lavishly entertained in economic, business, financial, political and military literature.

By contrast, the latter mode, that of acclimating to circumstances, seems to have escaped much attention except in poetic or religious works, or in biological studies of adaptive responses (e.g., the tanning of sun-exposed skin).

Natural selection, being non-teleological and operating by simply preventing procreation, is not an instance of the acclimation mode.

However, an individual who chooses to abandon one path because it does not pan out and to follow instead a path of less resistance or greater promise can be said to be employing this latter mode.

quotes for comparison

Wherever I found a living thing, there found I Will to Power; and even in the will of the servant found I the will to be master. It is not the river that is your danger and the end of your good and evil, ye wisest ones: but that Will itself, the Will to Power — the unexhausted, procreating life-will.

Friedrich Nietzsche
(1844-1900)
Thus Spake Zarathustra

59

Possible motives for our cultural emphasis on the control mode are numerous. First, we may prefer feeling "in control" of a situation rather than at the mercy of external forces, and wielding Influence may feel more "in control" than does adjusting Capacity.

Second, we tend to respect dominance — or even failed attempts at dominance — over submission, and we associate control with dominance and acclimation with submission.

Third, the former mode is typically much more immediate, externally visible and dramatic in its results than is the latter. This drama in turn elicits significantly more positive feedback from others.

For instance, if history and popular elections be any indication, one typically receives more fame and adoration for killing people in war (primarily control) than for learning to live with them in harmony (primarily acclimation).

Similarly, the inherent drama of "curing" problems (primarily control) rather than preventing them in the first place (primarily acclimation) — coupled with the difficulty of demonstrating when the latter approach has worked — cause us to overvalue the former, creating unequivocal financial incentives actually to promote rather than prevent problems. The cure-rather-than-prevent paradigm operates as a financial windfall for the medical and legal professions, for example.

Nonetheless, to master Wealth, we must recognize both modes as viable and valuable alternatives.

quotes for comparison

Receive my instruction, and not silver; and knowledge rather than choice gold. For wisdom is better than rubies; and all the things that may be desired are not to be compared to it.

The Proverbs (circa 6th-10th century B.C.)

60

Each choice reduces to a preference for acclimation, control, or some combination of both.

While it is impossible to determine *a priori* which mode is appropriate for any given situation, reference to priorities already established yields a principle:

When choosing whether to control or acclimate, that option offering the greatest likelihood of preserving and optimizing Capacity, empowering choice itself, and causing or allowing musts and wants actually to occur should be chosen.

As in the prospective equation of Wealth, this principle incorporates determinations of probability explicitly, which approach again comports with real-life: virtually no choice we make is guaranteed to produce the results we want.

Since risk of failure or unintended results is inherent in decision-making, consulting the appropriate body of state-of-the-art human knowledge and gathering as much situation-specific information as possible so as to make the most of our power of choice is vital.

Consequently, it is not mere rhetoric or hyperbole to say that knowledge is a component of Wealth and an essential component of Wealth mastery.

quotes for comparison

War therefore is an act of violence to compel our opponent to fulfill our will.

Violence, that is to say, physical force (for there is no moral force without the conception of States and Law), is therefore the MEANS; the compulsory submission of the enemy to our will is the ultimate object.

Karl von Clausewitz
(1780-1831)
On War

61

The control mode implies Influence, and, of the four factors of Wealth, Influence — particularly in the form of money — has received by far the most attention in modern Wealth-related literature. As a result, when the control mode is appropriate, vast bodies of knowledge are available to assist us in effectively wielding Influence.

For instance, political theorists and sociologists can teach us much about social influence, and their knowledge should be deployed accordingly.

Scientists and engineers can teach us much about physical influence over things and people, and their knowledge should be deployed accordingly.

Economists and businesspeople can teach us much about market transactions in appreciables and influenceables, and their knowledge should be deployed accordingly.

Law is the primary basis of many forms of social influence, such as property rights, and thus knowledge of the law should be deployed accordingly.

quotes for comparison

The highest goodness is like water. Water benefits all things and does not compete. It stays in the lowly places which others despise. Therefore it is near the Eternal.

Lao Tzu
(circa 500 B.C.)
Tao Te Ching

62

While the acclimation mode of choice implementation may receive less fanfare, its mechanisms — learning, growth, adaptation — are not unfamiliar to us at all.

Each time we learn a new vocabulary word, for instance, we are acclimating to our existing Environment by increasing a Capacity for beneficial Appreciation.

Each time we inoculate ourselves against disease, we are acclimating to our existing Environment by decreasing a Capacity for detrimental Appreciation.

One benefit of the acclimation mode is that it typically requires no consent from others. One can choose to learn a new skill or develop a flare for existing culture without having to seek anyone's approval. Moreover, the relative invisibility or delayed visibility of acclimation serves the purposes of the socially or politically vulnerable well.

The acclimation mode falls within the purview of education, psychology, religion, philosophy, art, medicine and the natural sciences. Individual development and transformation, however, tend to be much more eccentric, private and unpredictable processes than those of the control mode, and, as a result, techniques and information sources that serve one person well may serve another poorly.

quotes for comparison

For money enters in two different characters into the scheme of life. A certain amount, varying with the number and empire of our desires, is a true necessary to each one of us in the present order of society; but beyond that amount, money is a commodity to be bought or not to be bought, a luxury in which we may either indulge or stint ourselves, like any other. And there are many luxuries that we may legitimately prefer to it, such as a grateful conscience, a country life, or the woman of our inclination. Trite, flat, and obvious as this conclusion may appear, we have only to look round us in society to see how scantily it has been recognised; and perhaps even ourselves, after a little reflection, may decide to spend a trifle less for money, and indulge ourselves a trifle more in the article of freedom.

Robert Louis Stevenson
(1850-1894)
Familiar Studies of Men & Books

Part X

63

At the stage of choice implementation, the subject matter becomes more familiar: jobs, income, investments and the remaining material that fills literally thousands of financial planning and get-rich books, articles and seminars each year.

It also offers the opportunity to address topics typically treated as afterthoughts, so-called "quality of life" issues.

That common parlance treats wealth and quality of life as severable belies that "wealth" has become synonymous with the much narrower notion of "riches" and its formalistic counterpart, "net worth."

quotes for comparison

Power is a means to an end. The end is every thing, without exception, which the human being calls pleasure, and the removal of pain.

James Mill
(1773-1836)
An Essay on Government

64

When implementing a choice to control, a particular form or combination of forms of Influence is selected from those available.

Then this form or combination of forms of Influence is used to cause or allow an effect that is expected to result in a desired form of Appreciation.

Selecting the right tool to get the job done is the art of Influence.

It is *savoir faire* in the literal sense.

quotes for comparison

I love liberty, and I loathe constraint, dependence, and all their kindred annoyances. As long as my purse contains money, it secures my independence and exempts me from the trouble of seeking other money, a trouble of which I have always had a perfect horror; and the dread of seeing the end of my independence makes me proportionately unwilling to part with my money. The money that we possess is the instrument of liberty, that which we lack and strive to obtain is the instrument of slavery. Thence it is that I hold fast to what I have, and yet covet nothing more.

Jean Jacques Rousseau
(1712-1778)
The Confessions of J. J. Rousseau

65

Most control choices can be implemented through any of a broad array of alternative forms of Influence.

For instance, assume that one is seeking to Appreciate a particular appreciable: a beautiful home.

The most common modern approach would be to exchange certain property rights, in money, for other property rights, in real estate, so as to secure access to this appreciable. Such a market exchange is strictly an exchange of social influence, specifically, property rights.

These legal rights are in turn enforced through physical force — or at least the threat of it — wielded by others, namely, the police, the courts and sometimes even the neighbors.

Thus, once one gains ownership (social influence) that is recognized (appreciation) by others, they will use force (physical influence) if necessary to protect one's possession (appreciation) of the house (appreciable).

They will even voluntarily keep off (mental influence) the land (appreciable).

quotes for comparison

All state obligations, payment of taxes, fulfillment of state duties, and submission to punishments. . . to which people appear to submit voluntarily, are always based on bodily violence or the threat of it.

The basis of authority is bodily violence.

Leo Tolstoy
(1828-1910)
The Kingdom of God Is Within You

66

But a market exchange is by no means the only form of Influence that could get the job done.

Physical influence could be used directly to invade and take possession of the land by force.

This technique has been used by conquering hordes from ancient to modern times. The United States of America and the Roman Empire are but two of many civilizations that were largely founded — rightly or wrongly — upon this very approach.

An individual could try it, too. However, in absence of a general disintegration of society, physically taking someone else's home will not likely result in extended enjoyment of it. Those same people who would protect a purchaser's possession of the home in the first scenario will soon enough come dispossess the invader in the second scenario.

Nonetheless, the essential mechanism from a Wealth perspective, Influence, is at work in both the market exchange and the invasion scenarios.

quotes for comparison

Good gracious! Lord bless me! Only think! Dear me! Mr. Darcy! Who would have thought it! And is it really true? Oh! My sweetest Lizzy! How rich and how great you will be! What pin-money, what jewels, what carriages you will have! Jane's is nothing to it — nothing at all. I am so pleased — so happy. Such a charming man! — So handsome! So tall! — Oh, my dear Lizzy! Pray apologise for my having disliked him so much before. I hope he will overlook it. Dear, dear Lizzy. A house in town! Every thing that is charming! Three daughters married! Ten thousand a year! Oh, Lord! What will become of me. I shall go distracted.

Jane Austin
(1775-1817)
Pride and Prejudice

67

The scenarios continue. Another alternative would be to exert social influence in the form of reputation, communication and attractiveness to marry the legal owner of a beautiful home.

In fact, in times and cultures where women were denied property rights, this implementation was the highly preferred (if not the only) approach for women. It has undoubtedly been used knowingly and successfully millions of times and remains fully viable and commonplace today.

This scenario, like the first, leads to establishment of legal rights, thereby again invoking the power of the state and the neighbors should a trespasser appear.

Finally, social influence in the form of status may be deployed with equally happy results.

For instance, political offices, church positions and other institutional roles often come with housing privileges such that one can, through attainment of a certain status, rightfully enjoy a beautiful home without having to buy, invade or marry at all.

quotes for comparison

Good name in man and woman, dear my lord, is the immediate jewel of their souls. Who steals my purse steals trash; 'tis something, nothing; 'twas mine, 'tis his, and has been slave to thousands. But he that filches from me my good name robs me of that which not enriches him and makes me poor indeed.

William Shakespeare
(1564-1616)
Othello

68

Each of these combinations of forms of Influence are therefore very well-documented, alternative means for enjoying the same appreciable, a beautiful home. Yet every net worth statement includes money, and no net worth statement includes reputation, attraction, status, physical power or other forms of Influence.

Business accounting procedures do allow inclusion of reputation in the value of a company through trademark valuation, but, even if such an approach were applied to an individual (assigning a dollar value to an individual's rights of publicity, for instance), such a picture remains profoundly under-inclusive as a measure of Wealth.

One attempt in economics to fill such gaps has yielded the oxymoronic notion of "human capital."

In plutonomic analysis, there is no need to force such analogies: Influence on machines and on humans — and, in turn, *through their* Influence on machines and humans — is a means.

Humans wield such means.

quotes for comparison

Property is a general term for rules governing access to and control of land and other material resources. Because these rules are disputed, both in regard to their general shape and in regard to their particular application, there are interesting philosophical issues about the justification of property. Modern philosophical discussions focus mostly on the issue of the justification of private property rights (as opposed to common or collective property). "Private property" refers to a kind of system that allocates particular objects like pieces of land to particular individuals to use and manage as they please, to the exclusion of others (even others who have a greater need for the resources) and to the exclusion also of any detailed control by society.

Jeremy Waldron
"Property"
The Stanford Encyclopedia of Philosophy (Fall 2004 Edition)
Edited by Edward N. Zalta

Part XI
69

One possible explanation for the divide between that which does and that which does not get counted as Wealth in economics and finance lies in a particular tenet of Influence, its most starkly contrasting trait in comparison to Appreciation and Capacity: transferability.

Unlike Capacity and Appreciation, many forms of Influence can be transferred.

And these transferable forms of Influence happen to be the same forms of Influence that appear on a net worth statement, namely, property rights.

Meanwhile, the non-transferable forms of Influence — reputation, attractiveness, citizenship and the rest — are treated just like Capacity and Appreciation. They are omitted altogether.

The end result is exactly what exists: almost an entire culture that uses a subset of the forms of Influence as a measure of Wealth itself.

This viewpoint harms subscribers through omission of crucial factors that bear directly upon Wealth and Wealth management, namely:

— all forms of Capacity
— all forms of Appreciation
— many of the most important forms of Influence: status (including citizenship, organizational membership, and familial and tribal standing), reputation, communication, attractiveness and physical prowess

quotes for comparison

Figures often beguile me, particularly when I have the arranging of them myself; in which case the remark attributed to Disraeli would often apply with justice and force: "There are three kinds of lies: lies, damned lies and statistics."

Mark Twain
(1835-1910)
Autobiography of Mark Twain

70

A likely cause for the overemphasis of transferability may be termed precision bias.

Determination of a precise value for transferable Influence is extremely easy: the market sets the value. Even if this value is utter nonsense, as in the case of market bubbles, its dollars-and-cents precision is indisputable.

But non-transferable qualities are simply not susceptible to precise valuation, there being no market for, say, empathy.

As humans, we have a gargantuan preference for precision. Formulas, statistics, bureaucracy, red tape and "official" things — even if completely fraudulent — carry an air of indelible credibility and authority.

Meanwhile, imprecise and unquantifiable notions — even if indisputably real — are systematically and universally discounted or even disregarded entirely.

These biases are so ingrained, in fact, that the most important Wealth variables in our lives — health, interpersonal relationships, citizenship, freedom of choice — are assigned, through omission, an effective Wealth value of exactly 0.00 by the very professionals whose job it is to advise us regarding Wealth. If it were not so tragically sad and bizarre, precision bias would be funny.

Diversification
>Investing in a wide range of asset types so as to mitigate the overall risk inherent in a portfolio; the opposite of "putting all eggs in one basket."

Contemporary financial planners almost universally recommend diversifying one's investment portfolio to include some cash, some stocks, some bonds, some real estate, some precious metals, and/or a variety of other assets as well as taking defensive legal measures, such as trusts.

From an actual Wealth perspective, such "diversification" is precariously non-diverse. The good investor will not only put some resources into the narrow range of assets recommended by financial planners but also into more powerful investment vehicles, including:

- education
- marketable skill and professional license or certification
- personal reputation, "image" and appearance
- physical strength, agility and endurance
- aesthetic sensibility, taste, "class"
- family relationships
- friends
- business contacts
- creation of intellectual property
- church or other community participation and standing
- political or organizational membership and status
- peaceful, safe, clean and uplifting living and working conditions

However, no one gets a commission or a management fee for advising a client, "I can't help you; you should spend your time and money on a university degree or a professional networking group." On the contrary, a financial planner or stockbroker has a strong incentive to ensure that clients *don't* diversify.

Thus, if an individual wishes to achieve actual diversification, he or she will have to be relatively self-reliant in identifying and evaluating investment opportunities.

71

Another likely cause for overemphasis of transferability is self-interest, namely, the self-interest of *others*, and more specifically, those others who place their own interests above the interests of the person whose Wealth is under consideration.

No matter how wealthy one is, the only Wealth someone else can *take away* is the transferable Wealth. No one can take and use as their own another person's, say, writing skills.

But someone can take ownership rights to a house.

Thus, generally speaking, the only immediate, self-interested concern one person can have in the Wealth of another is in the second person's transferable Influence.

This reality explains why creditors want a net worth statement in standard net worth statement form. They only want transferable Influence. The rest is truly useless to them.

However, the fact that our non-transferable Wealth has no value to our creditors does not imply that such Wealth has no value to *us*.

quotes for comparison

In some fields of his country, there are certain shining stones of several colours, whereof the Yahoos are violently fond. And when part of these stones is fixed in the earth . . . they will dig with their claws for whole days to get them out; then carry them away, and hide them by heaps in their kennels; but still looking round with great caution, for fear their comrades should find out their treasure.

In the fields where the shining stones abound, the fiercest and most frequent battles are fought.

Jonathan Swift
(1667-1745)
Gulliver's Travels

72

As discussed, social influence is strictly dependent upon perception and the opinion of the perceiver.

A wheelbarrow full of authentic currency will not buy a sandwich when the issuing government has collapsed: we no longer believe in that money. Yet the worthless wheelbarrow contents may represent years of investment, sacrifice and labor.

Perception and opinion are themselves largely a product of our interactions with others, which raises the third probable reason why transferable Influence is mistaken for Wealth: conformity.

We may privately harbor a belief that "money can't buy happiness," but when those around us still pursue the former much more vigorously than the latter — or even to the detriment of the latter —, we cannot help but follow suit. In fact, we may feel coerced into money-grubbing just as a peace-preferring nation may feel coerced into an arms race by the presence of a warlike neighbor.

Nonetheless, money remains but one of many forms of Influence, and those who sacrifice more Wealth to gain money than the money so gained is worth are simply not being good — or even rational — investors.

Meanwhile, to the clever Wealth-seeker, omnipresence of the wealth-as-riches view presents an opportunity to pursue the bullfighter while others are dutifully chasing the red cape.

quotes for comparison

Water shapes its course according to the nature of the ground over which it flows; the soldier works out his victory in relation to the foe whom he is facing. Therefore, just as water retains no constant shape, so in warfare there are no constant conditions. He who can modify his tactics in relation to his opponent and thereby succeed in winning, may be called a heaven-born captain.

Sun-tzu
(4th Century B.C.)
The Art of War

Part XII

73

When implementing a choice to acclimate, we identify the forms of Appreciation to which we are adapting and then seek to optimize our corresponding appreciative Capacity.

If the Appreciation to which we are adapting is beneficial, we seek to maximize our receptiveness; if the Appreciation to which we are adapting is detrimental, we seek to minimize receptiveness.

Because acclimation typically takes longer to produce results, effective employment of this approach requires development of self-control, self-discipline and self-mastery as well as some vision or sense for the future.

quotes for comparison

It is obvious that the different kinds of habits based on training, education and discipline of any sort are nothing but a long chain of conditioned reflexes. We all know how associations, once established and acquired between definite stimuli and our responses, are persistently and, so to speak, automatically reproduced, sometimes even although we fight against them. For instance, in the case of games and various acts of skill, it is as difficult to abolish all sorts of superfluous movements as to acquire the necessary movements; and it is equally difficult to overcome established negative reflexes, i.e., inhibitions. Again, experience has taught us that a difficult task should be approached by gradual stages.

Ivan P. Pavlov
(1849-1936)
Conditioned Reflexes: An Investigation of the Physiological Activity of the Cerebral Cortex

74

Having decided to acclimate, we must then evaluate feasibility and tactics for adjusting the pertinent Capacity.

Some capacities or lacks thereof are basically immutable. A person may, for instance, be physically incapable of sight or hearing.

When we cannot change a corresponding Capacity, we look to adjust other capacities as coping or compensatory measures. Thus, a blind person may develop an ability to read braille.

In the case of capacities that are mutable, we seek the best technique for bringing about a change.

Techniques for changing Capacity are numerous and varied: taking a class, reading, listening, observing, taking medication, having an operation, seeing a therapist or pursuing any number of other paths to personal development, growth and change.

Although instances of rapid Capacity adjustment can be found (through administration of a drug, for instance), alterations to Capacity must typically be planned far in advance of the time at which they are needed. Thus, once an obstacle appears, many avenues for acclimation may have already closed long ago.

Accordingly, short-sighted decision-makers must learn to rely almost exclusively upon control choices.

quotes for comparison

Even pleasure and good fortune are not relished without vigor and understanding. "*Things are as is the mind of their possessor: to one who knows how to use them, they are good; to one who abuses them, ill.*"

Whatever the benefits of fortune are, they yet require a palate to relish them. It is fruition, and not possession, that renders us happy. "*Neither land nor brass nor gold removes fevers from the ailing body or cares from the mind. The possessor must be healthy, if he aspires to make good use of his wealth. To him who is greedy or fearful, his house and estate are as a picture to a blind man.*"

Michel de Montaigne
(1533-1592)
Essays
with quotations from Horace and Terence

75

An example of acclimation is particularly informative, as it also illustrates the jatallic nature of Capacity: two book lovers each have a book.

The first book lover has a book in English but speaks only French; the second has a book in French but speaks only English. Neither has the capacity to appreciate the appreciable in his or her possession.

To an economist, the solution is obvious: market exchange of the books, moving each book to a higher-valued use.

But there is another way to resolve the problem: imparting Capacity.

Specifically, the two book lovers can teach each other or independently learn English and French, respectively, such that the Capacity of each is acclimated to the appreciable in hand, achieving the desired Wealth result without any exchange of property rights or possessions.

Such an occurrence, where something is passed from one to another without a corresponding loss to the first, is an instance of jatalla.

quotes for comparison

I desire. . . to leave this one great fact clearly stated. THERE IS NO WEALTH BUT LIFE. Life, including all its powers of love, of joy, and of admiration.

John Ruskin
(1819-1900)
Ethics of the Dust

76

The jatallic imparting of Capacity happens literally hundreds of thousands of times in the span of a life.

In fact, virtually all of our Capacity is acquired through such events: the passing of genetic information, the conveyance of language and social skills, almost the entire complex of qualities that make us human. Such mechanisms are exactly how book lovers become book lovers, English speakers become English speakers, adults become adults, and humans become humans in the first place.

Meanwhile, differences in Capacity — particularly, capacities to appreciate — explain why one person can lead an enviable and wealthy life with few possessions while another can be impoverished even in the midst of great riches.

Yet Capacity and the imparting of Capacity are almost nowhere to be found in contemporary economic and financial literature purporting to address Wealth.

quotes for comparison

Socrates: *"The same things, in fact, are wealth or not wealth, according as a man knows or does not know the use to make of them? To take an instance, a flute may be wealth to him who is sufficiently skilled to play upon it, but the same instrument is no better than the stones we tread under our feet to him who is not so skilled. . . unless indeed he chose to sell it?"*

Critobulus: *"That is precisely the conclusion we should come to. . . . You seem to say, Socrates, that money itself in the pockets of a man who does not know how to use it is not wealth?"*

Socrates: *"And, I understand you to concur in the truth of our proposition so far."*

Xenophen
(430-355 B.C.)
The Economist

77

The absence of Capacity, Appreciation and most forms of Influence from modern Wealth-related literature may have its origins all the way back in the first lesson of Wealth.

When first exposed to the world, we are hardly in touch with the functions of our Capacity. Instead, we are but painfully and singularly aware of all the things we need, probably food and companionship being preeminent on the list. We are essentially oblivious to the many indispensable *receptors* and *controllers* we have for those things.

Perhaps as adults, when we seek to maximize our Wealth, we revert to that infantile perspective. The problem is that this mindset is quite distorted, and the variables it omits — discussed now at length — are crucial to accurate assessment of Wealth and informed Wealth decision-making.

If we decide simply to live with the gaps, we may well be disappointed with our Wealth and not understand what went wrong.

If, on the other hand, we hone our ability to make informed choices according to rational priorities, we may take conscious steps to bring ourselves and those around us the enjoyment of higher Wealth.

The rest belongs to fate, fortune or divine will.

Appendix

Poverty. Reviewers of the present work have requested a separate discussion of poverty. In plutonomic analysis, poverty simply signifies a relative absence of wealth. Like wealth, it is subjective, dynamic and contextual. To oversimplify, if we were to plot different levels of wealth along a bounded continuum, maximum wealth would serve as one endpoint, and utter poverty (short of death) would serve as the other.

As wealth is the occurrence of highly beneficial and desirable appreciation and influence, poverty is being denied the same. The wealthy person taps the benefits of many resources, pursues engrossing and meaningful activities, and enjoys deep friendships and community ties. The person in poverty is prevented from accessing vital resources, unable to act in conformity with his or her beliefs and desires, and unwillingly without companionship.

"Experts." Every generation believes that it is somehow special and different from the rest, that it is immune to error. But, as often as not, one era's expert is the next era's laughingstock. Not that long ago, the most educated and "knowledgeable" of our ancestors believed that the earth was flat, that the health of the human body depended upon a balance of four liquids (the humours — blood, choler, phlegm and black bile), and a wide variety of other myths that now strike us as ridiculous. But at the time, the proponents of such views were highly revered and powerful. Doubting such myths offered a shortcut to martyrdom.

Unless our generation really is the first to achieve omniscience, much if not most of what we believe today is also destined for ridicule, and those who are most sure of what they "know" — our "experts" — will come off as having been the most deluded. Some fields may be safer than others, but the fields in which we wrestle with the messiness of real, live beings living in the real world are particularly fertile ground for major mistakes.

Just as we today look back with horror and disbelief at cultures — not so long ago — that institutionalized slavery or burned "witches" at the stake, I think it is clear that future generations will shake their heads in amazement at many of our own practices. The irreversible devastation that our generation has wrought upon the earth and its other species is a shoo-in for such disgust. Our descendants will ask themselves what we were thinking, and our answer will be clear: we were not. We pretended to know so much about economics and finance, individual rights and liberties, democracy and capitalism. We did not.

Business. Once one has studied wealth, it is difficult to go back to reading literature based on currently prevailing economic and financial notions, many of which are almost certainly destined to join the four humours. I recently happened across a book that a friend was reading as part of his MBA program at a reputable business school. The first line of the first chapter of the book proudly proclaimed, "The purpose of a business is to make a profit."

Presumably, the authors felt that they were stating the obvious, a universal absolute. Indeed, to those of us raised in the West, their pronouncement is so unassailable that its truth need not even be demonstrated. It is true in the same way that the earth is flat.

The only problem is that the earth is round. Contrary to the above, the purpose of a business is to *generate wealth, namely, wealth for the owners, employees and customers as well as all other stakeholders (e.g., landlords, adjoining property owners, suppliers)*. It is completely possible — and common — to turn a profit while destroying wealth; activities that produce huge negative externalities, such as pollution, or that exhaust non-renewable resources embody this very approach. And it is similarly possible — and common — to generate wealth while not turning a profit; effective non-profit organizations do just that.

Generating wealth and making profit are

completely compatible, but the one does not imply the other. If a person achieves both, that's doing business. But making profit at the expense of one's own wealth is not rightly called business. It is more appropriately characterized as squandering, debasement, waste, pyrrhic victory, being penny-wise and pound-foolish, or just plain old stupidity. Meanwhile, making profit at the expense of the wealth of others is not business either; it is better construed as fraud, theft, swindling, embezzlement, larceny by trick, conversion, trespass, and the like.

In short, wealth is the touchstone, not profit. The latter without the former may be called "fool's profit."

Strange as it may seem to us now, thinkers of previous ages viewed profit-making as inherently immoral. While this extreme position may not be accurate, it seems no more extreme and no less accurate than the unqualified profit-worship that permeates modern business and economic thought.

Perhaps when the earth has been depleted of virtually all resources and rid of all species except humans and cockroaches, we will revisit the difference between wealth and profit.

GDP. Bad information gives birth to bad decisions. Unfortunately, fool's profit and similar fallacies are now embedded in many of the tools we use to make society-wide decisions. One of the most egregiously flawed tools is the measurement known as gross domestic product or GDP, which is almost universally considered to be the most comprehensive and "important" measurement of an economy. Under prevailing economic theory, economic growth is supposed to be good, and an increase in GDP is supposed to indicate economic growth. An increase in GDP is therefore supposed to be good.

Unfortunately, as a logical and mathematical matter, treating GDP growth as a good thing means that we may treat terrorism and natural disasters as good things. These catastrophes force us to incur huge expenses, and in that way boost GDP. In short, when the brilliant mathematicians of the 20th century invented GDP, all the things your kindergarten teacher said were bad — war, fire, floods, disease, crime — were magically transformed into good. It's really quite beautiful and poetic.

And perverse to the point of psychopathy.

Take some everyday examples: if boosting GDP is a good thing, then an illness costing $15,000 in treatment is *better* than health, which costs $0 to treat. Fifteen-thousand dollars better, to be exact, since the sickness treatment boosts GDP by that amount, while health goes completely unregistered in the market.

Change the example so that the $15,000 is spent on cigarettes. This expenditure also boosts GDP by $15,000, but keeping one's money — and one's lungs — has no impact.

Multiply the madness by several hundred million transactions per year, and, *voila*, you've got GDP, the world's most important measure of well-we're-not-really-sure-what. It's definitely not a measure of wealth, and it's definitely not even a measure of things we want to happen, unless illnesses, suicide bombers, car wrecks, and natural disasters are desirable.

In plutonomic analysis, by contrast, we take the radical position that war, fire, terrorism, cancer and floods are not good. They are the same old evils they were before economics came along.

Whatever GDP is, using GDP as a tool in our decision-making process may actually be worse than using no measurement at all. Even rain dances and divining rods look like high science alongside GDP-based reasoning: something that is merely worthless is, after all, superior to something that is patently psychopathic.

Capacity-mapping. A practical application of wealth theory, capacity-mapping is the essence of being a good manager or parent. Specifically, capacity-mapping consists of perceiving the capacities of an individual and then finding circumstances — schools, jobs, cities, neighborhoods, communities — that offer a blend of influenceables and appreciables that provide an optimal match for those capacities.

Decision-assistance software. While assigning universal pain and pleasure values may be impossible, prospects are much more promising for the profitable use of numerical values that are assigned to two different outcomes for the *same* individual. Computing power may help us succeed where previous generations failed. Through the use of a software interview mechanism and a scenario comparison engine accessible via Internet, information technology may enable unprecedented modes of analysis of wealth-related decisions, perhaps to the point where even die-hard net worth disciples would be willing to move forward.

Wealth data aggregation. Rather than replace GDP with just another measure of market activity — thereby leaving the central error fully intact —, actual wealth data submitted for the use of decision-assistance software can be collected and analyzed to identify wealth trends and to record the effects of natural and socio-political events.

Such data can then be used for more effective wealth-related decision-making on a collective level.

Acknowledgments

My ongoing dialog with Danielle Miller was not only entertaining and adventurous but also instrumental in shaping the present theory. The practical vision of Rebecca Weeks can be credited for whatever accessibility the text may have. Office manager Nicole Theiss was a wonderful ally throughout the process.

Working with the remainder of the group that made this publication possible was a pleasure: illustrator Jonathan Klemstine, layout designer Michael Ng, and cover designer Christopher Tjalsma.

Many thanks also go to Golnar Zahedin, Andy Willis, Colan Pursell, Nancy Stone, Colby Hollifield, Julian Colbeck, Brad Conder, Tom Brown, Ellis Haguewood, Norman Thompson, Jim Russell, Terry Shelton, Sherry Rosenwein, Steve and Katka Werth, Jeff Werlwas, Loyal Murphy, Michael Lynch, Juliet Attalla, Vit Henisz, Sterritt Armstrong, Stacy Wray and Gus Austin, Rebecca Nelson, Todd Reese, Rob Fisher, Christina Linhardt, and Brucene, Shelton and Camille Harrison.

About the Author

S. E. Harrison teaches law, logic, writing, and reading comprehension in Los Angeles, California.